If we could fly

Karen Armstrong
If we could fly

If we could fly
ISBN 978 1 76041 108 4
Copyright © text Karen Armstrong 2016
Cover from a painting by Karen Armstrong

First published 2016 by
GINNINDERRA PRESS
PO Box 3461 Port Adelaide 5015 Australia
www.ginninderrapress.com.au

Contents

You are in need of me	9
Sitting in your car	10
Discussing chemo	11
The Walrus and the Carpenter wait with us	13
Nothing spoils your day	14
Friendship with strings attached	15
In the chemo suite	16
We chased the wind	17
A short history lesson	18
We tried the trees	19
Our teachers	20
Just having fun	21
A question of fear	22
No more make-believe	23
Who will tell the children?	24
All gone now	25
Tongue-tied	26
Formless	27
Decked in full armour	28
Pocket-sized hero	29
With a little help	30
A parable of anger	31
When anger comes	32
Just like a child	33
It's the little things	34
Empty confusions	35
Always they come	36
The power of a badge	37
A canine impersonation	38
In the silence: Haydn's Farewell Symphony No. 45	39
Like a prayer	40
What to do?	41
Another day on the ward	42
Nothing works	43

The art of repetition	44
About a Rosary	45
Widdershins	46
Overwhelmed	47
My side of the curtain	48
Written between the lines	49
In need of a good book	50
My faith is tested	51
A higher force	52
When seasons change	53
Not interested	54
Our dark animal	55
When we are gone	56
It's in the voice	57
It's all about feathers	58
Instructions for a contemporary ghost	59
You comforted me	60
Keeping it simple	61
On the outgoing tide	62
Life wills out	63
We all go back	64
Useless now	65
Quelling the fever	66
Outside your window	67
All that a son can do	68
If we could fly	69
While I am gone	70
Letting go	71
Everybody smiles today	72
Your last question	73
The balance of your hours	74
A snap decision	75
Contrast	76
After your passing	77
Leaving you	78

This book is dedicated to my friend Regina Betzold (Reggy),
Andrew, Darren, Alana, Rebecca and James, the children
and grandson she loved beyond all else.

And to all who, with love, have shared or are sharing
our final earthly journey.

Also for Carli, Ben and the grandchildren I will treasure.

Time after time,
like day the body dies.

Time after time, the night is newly born
awash with stars.

You are in need of me

Last night I dreamed
that I dreamed a dream of you.

You were a spectral form
drifting around the edges of my rabbit hole.

Softly, softly whispering
   softly, softly calling
      my name.

Sitting in your car

Remember the day we parked
beneath the river birches?

The creek crystal in the sun,
autumn's scent all around us.

We each recalled lives
spent thrashing against the tide.

We reached shore safely every time.

Discussing chemo

Your feet devastated by diabetes
you could no longer descend the slope to my front door.

After the appointment we sat in your car at the top of the drive,
each renewing our best-friend promises.

The more we spoke
the more our words melded

into tiny spheres of hope
which whirled and danced in the darkening air around us.

The 1812 Overture and nobody to talk to

Your doctor stilled our tongues
with medi-speak.
Now, I smile and wave
as you drive away, unaware
that Death is making faces
from the backseat.
Down my street a dog barks
frenetically, maddeningly.
Tchaikovsky's cannons boom
inside my head.
Dread drags and drags,
truth snaps like brittle sunlight.
I tear into my garden,
shredding wild roses,
ripping up marigolds
and forget-me-nots.
I'd run to our priest
but he's far into
his dotage and fast asleep.
I'd chance calling on Heaven
if I were assured that God,
for one transcendent moment
could remember my name.

The Walrus and the Carpenter wait with us

Lewis Carroll

We're edgy
the taxi driver
was demented.
We're seated in spine-cracking chairs.

We're edgy,
you worry the broken zip on your handbag.
I assiduously investigate
machine-embroidered flowers adorning my flimsy skirt.

The oncologist's door remains firmly latched.
We know
      that the time has come to speak
        of ships and shoes and sealing wax,
         to ask why the sea is boiling hot
          or if pigs indeed have wings.
  The time has come.
    Too soon.

Nothing spoils your day

Why don't you kick, scream,
rail against fate?

I could fashion vowels and consonants
into comforting stanzas, swaddle you.

Instead we chuckle about nursing days
your scratchy starched caps, my ludicrous paper fold-ups.

To your mind it's no more than a day.
A day clad in a summer breeze

not to be spoiled by oncologists,
chemo referrals or this interminable wait for a taxi.

Friendship with strings attached

Dawn's first grey streaks settle over the low hills.
I stir my tea, trying to recall yesterday's moment
when you tied imperceptible string around my toes.

It's length stretched down the long, long road
from your house, across the creek and way up to
the top of my valley.

The string that you jerked the moment you woke
wrenching me from my bed

to make your eight a.m. first chemo
that I swore my sleepy head couldn't do until ten.

In the chemo suite

All is quiet,
nurses drift from drip to drip.
Chemo recipients doze or try and fail to focus
on crossword puzzles, reading.

We speak quietly about everything and nothing;
about taxi drivers with bad attitudes,
podiatrists with non-feet-friendly entrance ways,
the price of food from the kiosk

until you tire and rest back,
gazing out the window, tree-dreaming.

Your special nurse brings me
a more comfortable visitor's chair.

She knows I've signed on for the long haul.

We chased the wind

Winds were near gale force
the morning we drove to the edge of the lake.
Our talk drifted back to motorcycle days.
Days when wind whipped our hair,
stung our eyes and our bikes purred
like huge cats between our thighs.
Days when time was never-ending
and the sun, moon and stars
illuminated a world
that existed for us
and us alone.

A short history lesson

In the sixties and seventies
sex with new acquaintances
or strangers was
> just another way of saying hello.

You're right,
I should have said hello more often.

We tried the trees

No matter how many seeds we planted,
   how lovingly we tended them
      we never grew a money tree.

Our teachers

Gurus crossed our paths
to teach us
how not to know that we exist

so that when we die
we will not know
that we are dying.

Just having fun

Look at us.
Two giggledygerts

toying with the controls of your electric bed,
splashing cheap perfume.

Laughter is obligatory
when confronting cancer
        stage four.

A question of fear

If you were to ask
my thoughts or fears I could not answer.

I only know that failing sunlight
trickles through cracks in the clouds.

Blue gums beyond the fence
are greying ghosts with spindly arms.

And a giant fist has ripped out my heart,
night is coming.

No more make-believe

If only we were children
playing hospital

but death brooks no pretence,
reality cuts my bones
and I want to bolt.

Sharp-suited professors,
overworked nurses
and fashion-plate doctors
leave a frenzy of questions
smouldering in your grey eyes.

Don't look to me, I'm
a long-ago nurse
and present-day friend
who hasn't a clue.

You wake laughing after a dream
from way back when you chased
your nude children along the shoreline.

I will stay,
stay
   and do all that a friend can do.

Who will tell the children?

I have accompanied you to doctors,
read your blood markers.

It's too late.

You blithely deny the beast,
we're alone.

Your adult children walk in ignorance
for I am voiceless.

All gone now

I'm so late, I've been stalking shadows,
sugar coating realities,

untangling cobwebs spun from good intentions
rolling up clapped-out nightmares

and all our dirty linen
now hangs sparkling on the line.

Tongue-tied

I dare not mouth a word,
gibberish will spill from my lips.

Your doctor might think I'm speaking in tongues
and revere me as holy.

Formless

Thoughts are clear, vague shapes
suspended in the air between us

like half-finished balloons
cast aside by a glass-blower.

Decked in full armour

I woke with the birds,
set to slay dragons for you.

All through the day
I parried and thrust

but the beasts smacked me down,
laying waste to my armour, incinerating my sword.

Blanketed in ash I rest by your bed,
ruing this day.
Incurably baffled by a world
that declines all requests to cease spitting fire.

Pocket-sized hero

You extol my virtues,
laud my name to all and sundry.

I'm no hero.
All day, everyday I dig with tiny, shiny shovels
hunting for courage enough
not to renege on a promise.

With a little help

That angry Monday
you were short of expletives
so we put our heads together.

Pianissimo
we fuck-worded
and fuck-worded
those tumours to death.

A parable of anger

Anger, blame or self-recrimination were not your forte,
until manic Monday.

That day I hared around
reassembling doctors, nurses

any unfortunate felled
by the frenzy of missiles shot from your tongue.

Afterward you donned a metaphorical hair shirt
that refused to fit.

I hauled it away.

When anger comes

The house of your spirit
is self-destructing brick by brick.

Don't apologise for
for this small anger

I won't unravel
like an old woollen sock.

Thread by thread
I'm striving to be stronger that.

Just like a child

She's afraid, Andrew,
incapable of wrapping us in love.

She's afraid, Andrew.
Do you remember dreading the dark,
monsters in the cupboard
or bogeymen who could swallow you whole?

She's scared like that, Andrew.
Demons lurk in darkness
darker than darkness.
She's scared, Andrew.

We were all children.
Year by year, decade by decade
we grew, we aged, but deep within our core
the-child-that-was holds fast.

Andrew, the blood of that child
is running cold, Andrew. Cutting cold.

It's the little things

Our little fates
weigh heavy like held-back breaths.

My hands gesture loss,
balance emptiness.

I could close my eyes,
blot out this room.

Other worlds await us.

Empty confusions

Stuck to the seat
of your bedside chair, I see

all that's here,
nothing that isn't here.

Could it be that nothing is here at all
and I'm seeing it anyway?

Always they come

I woke you from a light sleep.
You didn't speak but you smiled
and your smile was beautiful.

We sensed a disturbance
in the air around us

we had predicted the advent of angels.

The power of a badge

Your eyes scream grey fire.
You can't move,
can barely breathe.

You've called and called,
nobody answers.

Wielding my old registration badge
like a machete,
I reel in doctors and nurses.

Painkillers materialise
like a swift fall of wedding-day rice.

A canine impersonation

I've been busy,
busy impersonating a demented puppy
snapping at nurses' heels, barking down doctors' excuses.

Finally, needs met, you sleep
while I settle between the arms
of your bedside chair

to open a journal filled with hopes,
wishes and muddle-headed musings
for none to see but me.

In the silence: Haydn's Farewell Symphony No. 45

Hospital silence is insufferable.

I breathe in four-part fugues,
counterpoint harmonies
rub noise on my skin.

You sleep on and on.

Unaware that your beautiful life is
                      la Symphonie d'Adieu

Like a prayer

We're a sight, you dipping in and out
of consciousness, me to and fro
to the kitchen for hit after hit of sweet tea.

As if the jiggling of tea bags,
and the swirling clink-clink of a spoon

whipping the inside of a hospital cup
were a blessed sacrament
           in search of a miracle.

What to do?

I try to read
but the rhythm of your dying blurs the print.

If I speak my
syllables creak like rusty hinges.

Writing causes phrases
to fall screaming from my pen.

I settle back, unfolding
and refolding an unsightly muddle of introspections

while I pray a bucketful of prayers.

Another day on the ward

I dipped into a mystery novel
but the plot was lost on me.

I counted stitches in hospital blankets,
holes in the ceiling vent, losing count repetitively.

I spoke but my words were swallowed
as gospel or mistaken for promises.

Now I am settled by the window in a ward
scented with antiseptic and loss.

Prayerfully, painstakingly
crafting origami cranes

from finely cut, diligently collected
strips of sunlight.

Nothing works

Banishing my watch
failed to halt the passing hours.

My reiki light cannot reach
the severing cord nor heal the riven ends.

I dreamed you back to health
only to find that cancer refused to sleep.

I joined you in denial's gilded halls
but the walls buckled, collapsed

and all the windows imploded
shredding me with knives of glass.

The art of repetition

Again and again you wake,
again and again you ask,

What are you doing?

I could tell you
that I am not devising one hundred and one ways
to eat a grape.

I could tell you
that I am not counting filaments
in yellow vinyl floor stripes.

Or contemplating over and over
the memorial plaques inset
on the framed pictures in the corridor.

I could tell you so much that I am not doing
but the moment is lost, you fall straight back to sleep.

About a Rosary

From my window the morning appears still,
not a breath of wind.

Yet ribbons of drifting cirrus have banded
to form a crucifix in the sky
above the hospital where you are lying.

The Queen of Heaven cries out
from my bedside drawer.

Widdershins

When you were first hospitalised
I couldn't walk through the entrance

until I prayed the Lord's Prayer,
recited ten Hail Marys, spun widdershins
and counted to twenty.

Now I need no ritual or incantation,
I do doorways so well.

Overwhelmed

Your children, your therapists search me for guidance.
Common sense slammed her door
in my face and shot the bolt.

Home-spun wisdom wound herself
into a ball and rolled away.
Reason has risen above my reach.

Platitudes and clichés disintegrate
like brittle photos. Enlightened phrases
tangle wildly in my hair.

I beat a path to the kitchen, hunting up tannin.
With my lips assiduously sipping tea,
nobody expects a word from me.

My side of the curtain

Cheery-faced,
soft-shoe shod they float in and out.
Nurses, doctors,
cleaners and tea ladies,
opening and reopening your blue curtain.
I close it back.
Privacy is an out-and-out must
while I hum lullabies to nothingness
and pluck rusty strings on a long-ago guitar.

Written between the lines

I cart this two-for-five-dollars book everywhere.
It comforts me.

You are the black ink, thousands of words
and grey-eyed smile tucked within the pages.

In need of a good book

Although friendship's bond holds fast,
vigils can be tedious.
Should I insult the spirit
of balladeers worldwide
with this ancient copy of Pam Ayres?
Should I assault my synapses
with the forensic complexities
of a serial killer whodunnit?
Should I sing the blues with Sylvia Plath
or snuggle between the comforting paragraphs
of this timely find, a slim paperback treatise on life after life?

My faith is tested

If there be God I'll strip Him from Heaven,
if there be angels I'll shred their wings
and rip the stars from the firmament.

I'm strung out, wrung out, hung out, cried out.
I want to kick and scream
but my actions would be as nothing.

Death's holed up in the corner,
ridiculing my grandiose intentions.

A higher force

I have prayed, begged, bargained and beseeched.

Still
  if I ask the Lord one more time

you will wake, laugh and apologise for all this fuss.

  Only one more prayer.

When seasons change

All my life
I have been an incredulous child
when winter yields to spring,

when butterflies kiss the warming breeze
and bees fly off shod in tiny golden slippers.

Now I curse the season
that sprouted seeds
which will flower with your death.

Not interested

If old mother moon pitched from the sky,
performed delicate pliés and arabesques by my bed
while star points etched smiley faces
on my windowpanes.

I wouldn't care.
    You're leaving me.

Our dark animal

The low howl of a black dog
echoes through the crawl spaces of my mind.

A small, constant beast
who has tracked our solitary hours,
indelibly marked our days.

I will be shot of him before you wake.

When we are gone

In this hospital room, I doze
or count your every breath.

Two floors down strangers tread
footpaths where together we once walked.

Across the street others lunch in gardens
where we spun stories, shared secrets –

where time after time we laughed
and on a not-so-long-ago day, we cried.

Will sun-drenched pavements,
majestic oaks and gentle elms remember

our lazy footfall,
trivial profanities, irreverent absurdities?

Will particles or souls
remember the names we were given –
                the air we breathed?

It's in the voice

Your lips are parched
from chemo-thirst.

Near breathless you grasp the triangle
to hitch yourself up.

You're a mess,
a pain-drenched wreck.

   Yet your voice is smiling.

It's all about feathers

No amount of drugs blunt this misery.
        You half open your eyes, try to mouth words.

I incline my head as you raise your less-swollen hand–
        your touch is weightless
            febrile feathers against my cheek.

You ask why pain causes memories and dreams
            to scatter like dandelion puffs.

Instructions for a contemporary ghost

Should you find a way to evade
the guardians at Heaven's gate
should you find a way
to grace my home
with a haunting
don't wear white sheets,
dusty shrouds or grey nightgowns.
Dazzle me with a luminous haze
of gold, vermilion or magenta.
Forget diabetic boots and old-lady fluffies.
Bejewel your slender feet
with the lustre of pearls
and the brilliance of sapphires.
Thread my nights with laughter
and the fire of stars.
By day enfold me
in webs of secrets and harmonies
woven beyond the wild, incomprehensible spaces
of the Universe.

You comforted me

While you were dreaming I moved my chair
close to rest my head on the edge of your bed.
You woke and reached out your hand
to stroke my hair as if soothing a child.
Tears held off until
you drifted back
into the sleep
of a woman
set to soar
on the wings
of Thanatos.

Keeping it simple

In this room there will be no deathbed
proclamations. No priests or bouquets.

Here your body will lessen,
this life will end.

But you will die cocooned
in the love of your children
and one nonplussed but constant friend.

On the outgoing tide

The tide is rising.
You were never mine to keep.

I must speed walk
twenty city blocks,
hunt up a priest,
seek out a Buddhist temple,
light one thousand candles
and find a mountain
high enough
from which to scream.

On my return
we will breathe
the tang of warmed sourdough
and wild honey.

Life wills out

My only child was born on a day akin to this
when a golden sun drifted in the arms of a lazy sky.

Why am I seated on this courtyard bench,
calling up moments of unstinting joy?

Two floors up your name
fades faster and faster from this world.

We all go back

You sleep mouth-breathing,
pale lips
almost invisible.

My mind winds back to childhood,
to lying flat in sea-green grass,
arms and legs akimbo, mouth wide

catching rain.

Useless now

I fetched a tiny bag of lavender
to calm
to soothe.

Your pain screams
beyond the balm of herbs
and homespun remedies.

Outside the window,
thousands of fragrant seeds
trail a high summer breeze

Quelling the fever

I sponged you.

Soaked you in a frenzy of water.

Convinced beyond reason
that I could stay Death's hand
              with wet paper rags.

Outside your window

Deep within lacy cloud shadows
death birds circle and circle.

In their wake
        one snow-white dove.

All that a son can do

He gently syringed tiny drops
of clear juice into your parched mouth.

Swabbed your cracked lips
with wet cotton sticks.

No mouth care in this ward.

Except by once-upon-a-time nurses and loving sons.

If we could fly

Ceilings lower,
inch by inch and walls close in.

If I could beguile the wings off a seraph,
we would soar above the rock-strewn galaxies,
past birthing stars and icy planets
        to lands of legend
            lands beyond time
           beyond pain
            beyond death.

While I am gone

I must away.
Exhaustion hangs like a laden sky
and my aches refuse to be silenced.

Should old-fella death come courting,
don't accept his first embrace.

Tease, torture and torment him
until you're ready
to be lifted from this earthly cage of dreams.

Letting go

You asked
> What if chemo doesn't work?

I replied
> We will cross that bridge if we come to it.

Now that bridge rises before us,
  we must free your dreaming spirit
    so you can cross alone.

Everybody smiles today

Smiling
   you are dying smiles
    we will nurse you kindly smiles.

Madame Morphia finally knocked you flat.
Solicitude is lost on you now.

Your last question

I stretched up and across your high bed
to hear your lowering, ever lowering voice.

You asked
  Will it be sorted in the morning?

I promised it would.

The balance of your hours

These final hours dissolve
like rainbows into blue.
The tethering cord is severing.
You will bequeath this world to us
        before another morning wakes.

A snap decision

Your adult children
had turned away momentarily,
brother and sister hooking memories.

You left when neither gaze
nor hand reached towards you.

How like you to run with your heart.
    How like you to go it alone.

Contrast

Uninvited cancer roared in,
shredding us
with screaming wings of fire.

Death was a shy guest,
arriving on soft-soled shoes
to whisper you home.

After your passing

All is tranquil now,
affliction and pain vanquished.

With a brush of pink to your cooling lips
you could be merely sleeping and so, so young.

So kind of death to smooth our years away.

Leaving you

Earthly possessions packed,
your lifeless body lies serene.

With love
we turn away.

To catch the thread of lives
unstitched when the dying began.

To live
    because living is all
        that the living know how to do.

www.ingramcontent.com/pod-product-compliance
Lightning Source LLC
Chambersburg PA
CBHW062149100526
44589CB00014B/1753